The Village

by April De Angelis

after *Fuenteovejuna* by
Lope de Vega

First performed at Theatre Royal Stratford East
Friday 7 September 2018

Theatre Royal Stratford East
Gerry Raffles Square
London
E15 1BN

www.stratfordeast.com

The Village

April De Angelis

Cast

(in alphabetical order)

Harki Bhambra	Gopi
Sudha Bhuchar	Ishani
Anya Chalotra	Jyoti
Ameet Chana	Mango
Neil D'Souza	Ramdev
Souad Faress	Gina
Rina Fatania	Panna
Naeem Hayat	Vihaan
Scott Karim	Farooq
Art Malik	The Inspector
Arian Nik	Mekhal / Babu
Humera Syed	Jacinta
Ragevan Vasan	Ved

National Youth Theatre Chorus

Sofia Cala, Analise Dias, Humaira Iqbal,
Lauren Leppard, Roberta Livingston,
Zara Ramtobhul-Akbur, Ella Shire, Yasmin Twomey

Musicians

Violin, Harmonium, Vocals
Nawazish Ali-Khan

Bansuri Robinkumar R Christian

Percussion Keval Joshi

Original Play	Lope de Vega
Writer	April De Angelis
Director	Nadia Fall
Designer	Joanna Scotcher
Lighting Designer	Paul Pyant
Movement Director	Polly Bennett
Composer	Niraj Chag
Sound Designer	Helen Atkinson
Fight Directors	Rachel Bown-Williams, Ruth Cooper-Brown of RC Annie
Assistant Director	Emma Baggott
Hindi Lyricist & Songs Teacher	Japjit Kaur
Casting Director	Amy Ball
Literal Translator	Simon Scardifield
Research Consultant	Anish Ahluwalia
Production Manager	Richard Parr
Company & Stage Manager	Sarah Buik
Deputy Stage Manager	Zo Elsmore
Assistant Stage Manager	Rachel Rieley
Costume Supervisor	Natasha Prynne
Assistant Costume Supervisor	Finlay Forbes-Gower
Wardrobe Manager	Helen Charters
Dressers	Holly Layne-Hawkins, Georgia Pritchard
Head of Lighting	Laura Curd
Lighting Deputy	Deanna Towli
Lighting Programmer	Ed Locke
Head of Sound	Jeremy George
Sound No. 2	Patrick Ball
Head of Stage	Timothy Kelly-Trotman
Deputy Stage	Liam Roughley
NYT Chorus Coordinator	Lauren Buckley
Scenic Artists	Sarah Jo Evans, Emilie Mellor
Workshop Carpenter	Dominic Kelly
Work Placement, RADA	Victoria Murphy

Set built by Theatre Royal Stratford East Workshop

Thank you to: Creative Technology for Sound Hires, Sparks Theatrical for Lighting Hires, Sallyanne Dicksie

Cast Biographies

Harki Bhambra
Theatre includes: *Object Love* (Dissolve Theatre); *Mind The Gap* (Unity Theatre). TV includes: *Our Girl* Series 3, *Two Doors Down*, *Hospital People*, *Drifters*, *Doctor Who*, *Londongrad*.

Sudha Bhuchar
Theatre includes: *Lions and Tigers* (Shakespeare's Globe); *Khandan* (Birmingham Rep/Royal Court); *A Fine Balance* (Tamasha/Hampstead); *Haroun and The Sea of Stories* (National Theatre). Sudha last performed at Stratford East in *House of The Sun* (Tamasha). TV: *Coronation Street*, *Casualty*, *Holby City*, *The Living and The Dead*, *Doctors*, *The Enfield Haunting*, *Vera*, three series of *Stella*. Film includes: *Happy New Year Colin Burstead*, *Mary Poppins Returns* and *The Magnificent Eleven*.

Anya Chalotra
Anya is a recent graduate of Guildhall School of Music and Drama. Theatre includes: *Much Ado About Nothing* (Shakespeare's Globe). TV includes: *Wanderlust*, *Sherwood*, *The ABC Murders*.

Ameet Chana
Theatre includes: *What Shadows* (Edinburgh Lyceum/Park Theatre); *Anita & Me* (Birmingham Rep/Theatre Royal Stratford East); *Happy Birthday Sunita* (Watford Palace/UK and international tour); *The Djinns of Eidgah* (Royal Court); *Wicked, Yaar!*, *Voices in the Wind* (National Theatre); *Skeleton* (Soho). TV includes: *Doctors*, *Casualty*, *EastEnders*, *Holby City*, *The League of Gentlemen*, *The Accused*. Film includes: *Trendy*, *The Black Prince*, *Jab Tak Hai Jaan*, *Run, Fat Boy, Run*, *Bend It Like Beckham*.

Neil D'Souza
Theatre includes: *Beginners* (Unicorn Theatre); *The Hypocrite*, *Much Ado About Nothing*, *Midnight's Children* (RSC); *Skeleton* (Soho); *How to Hold Your Breath*, *Khandan* (Royal Court); *Herge's Adventures of Tintin* (West End); *The Man of Mode* (National Theatre); *Twelfth Night* (West End).

TV includes: *Humans, In the Long Run, Informer, Thanks for the Memories, EastEnders, Not Safe for Work, Citizen Khan, Friday Night Dinner, Doctors, Hustle, Holby City.* Film includes: *Filth, Still Life, Closed Circuit, Jadoo, Another Me, Wild Target.*

Souad Faress

Theatre includes: *Goats* and *A Curse* (Royal Court); *Chilcot* (The Lowry/BAC/NT Studios); *The House of Bernada Alba* (Almeida); *The Permanent Way* (Out of Joint/Sydney Theatre Company/National Theatre Company); *Homebody/Kabul* (Cheek by Jowl/Young Vic). TV includes: *Game of Thrones, Apple Tree House, Brief Encounters, Berlin Station, Sense8, Cabbage and Patch, Vera, Making of a Lady, Utopia, Hunted, Silent Witness, Holby City, Law and Order, Sarah Jane Adventures.* Film includes: *Christopher Robin, Bridget Jones's Baby, My Beautiful Launderette, Bhaji on the Beach* and *Twelfth Happiness.*

Rina Fatania

Theatre includes: *The Tin Drum* (Kneehigh); *Oliver Twist* (Regents Park, Open Air Theatre); *Roller Diner* (Soho); *Anita and Me* (UK tour); *Sinbad the Sailor, Love 'n' Stuff* (Theatre Royal Stratford East); *Dead Dog in a Suitcase* (Kneehigh/international tour); *The Empress* (RSC); *Wah! Wah! Girls* (Sadler's Wells/UK tour); *Britain's Got Bhangra* (UK tour); *Dick Whittington* (Hackney Empire). TV includes: *Wanderlust* (BBC/Netflix); *People Just Do Nothing* (BBC). Film includes: *Raabta, Digital-Mummji Presents, Mumbai Charlie, Travel Londoner.*

Naeem Hayat

Theatre includes: *Sonnet Walks, The Captive Queen,* Globe 2 Globe world tour of *Hamlet* (Shakespeare's Globe), *Faster-Higher-Stronger-Straighter* (Dominion Studio). Film includes: *Duperie, Undercliffe.*

Scott Karim

Theatre includes: *The Country Wife* (Chichester Festival Theatre); *Young Marx* (Bridge Theatre); *Imogen, The Merchant of Venice* (Shakespeare's Globe); *King Lear, Brave New World* (Royal & Derngate/UK tour); *The Invisible* (Bush Theatre); *Dara, Great Britain, Othello* (National Theatre). TV includes: *Electric Dreams, Britannia, Holby City.*

Art Malik
Theatre includes: *A Man for All Seasons*, *Equus* (Liverpool Playhouse); *Aliens* (Soho); *Art* (Wyndham's); *Cymbeline*, *Great Expectations* (Royal Exchange); *Destiny*, *Timon of Athens* (Bristol Old Vic); *Heroes* (UK tour); *Indian Ink* (Aldwych); *Othello* (RSC); *Romeo and Juliet*, *The 88 Prospect*, *The Government Inspector* (Old Vic); *The Seagull* (Royal Court/Broadway), *Trial Run* (Young Vic). TV includes: *The Jewel in the Crown*, *The Woman in White*, *Bancroft*, *Sherlock IV*, *Coldfeet*, *Goodness Gracious Me*, *Indian Summers*, *Homeland*, *Borgia*, *New Tricks*, *Upstairs Downstairs*, *Poirot*, *Lewis*. Film includes: *Passage to India*, *True Lies*, *Halal Daddy*, *Diana*, *Bhaag Mikha Bhaag*, *John Carter*, *Ghosted*, *Mirzya*, *Wolfman*, *Franklyn* and *The Living Daylights*.

Arian Nik
Theatre includes: *The Ugly One* (Park Theatre), *The Last Testament of Lillian Bilocca* (Hull Truck). Film includes: *Disney's Artemis Fowl*.

Humera Syed
Theatre includes: *The Arabian Nights* (Royal Lyceum Theatre); *Anita and Me* (tour).

Ragevan Vasan
Theatre includes: *Hurling Rubble at the Sun/Moon* (Park Theatre); *Love for Love*, *Queen Anne* (RSC). TV includes: *Save Me*, *Fortitude*, *The State*, *Cuffs*, *Doctors*. Film includes: *Tim Burton's Dumbo*, *Walk Like a Panther*, *Daphne*, *The Last Witness*.

Creative Team Biographies

April De Angelis | Writer

April is an acclaimed writer whose extensive theatre work includes *After Electra, Gastronauts, Jumpy*, an adaptation of *Frankenstein, My Brilliant Friend, Wuthering Heights, A Laughing Matter, A Warwickshire Testimony, The Positive Hour, Playhouse Creatures* and *The Life and Times of Fanny Hill*. Other credits: *Flight* (libretto) and *The Silent Twins* (libretto). Radio: an adaptation of *Life in the Tomb*, a serialisation of *Peyton Place, Visitants* and *The Outlander*. TV includes: *Aristophanes*.

Nadia Fall | Director

Nadia trained at Goldsmiths College (MA Directing) and on the NT Studio's Directors programme. Theatre includes: *The Suicide, Our Country's Good, Dara, Chewing Gum Dreams, Home, Untold Stories (Hymn); The Doctor's Dilemma* (National Theatre); *Hir, Disgraced* (Bush Theatre); *Way Upstream* (Chichester Festival Theatre); *Hobson's Choice* (Regent's Park Open Air Theatre). As Associate Director: *The Curious Incident of the Dog in the Night-Time* (Gielgud); *Collaborators, The Habit of Art* (National Theatre).

Joanna Scotcher | Designer

Theatre includes: *Emilia* (Shakespeare's Globe); *Winter* (Young Vic); *Katie Roche* (Abbey Theatre, Dublin); *Boys Will Be Boys* (Headlong, Bush Theatre); *Cuttin' It* (Young Vic, Royal Court); *The Railway Children* (National Railway Museum/King's Cross Theatre); *The Rolling Stone, Anna Karenina* (Royal Exchange); *A Harlem Dream* (Young Vic, Dance Umbrella); *Pests* (Royal Court, Royal Exchange); *Hopelessly Devoted* (Paines Plough); *Billy the Girl* (Clean Break, Soho).

Paul Pyant | Lighting Designer

Paul trained at Royal Academy of Dramatic Art (RADA) in London and for 45 years has been working in opera, ballet, musicals and theatre worldwide including the West End and on Broadway. Recent productions include: *Love in Idleness* (Menier/Apollo); *Lettice and Lovage* (Menier); *Julius Caesar* (Bristol Old Vic); *Hamlet* (RADA); *Annie Get Your Gun* (Det Ny Theatre); *The York Realist* (Donmar Warehouse); *Curtains* (Rose Theatre, Kingston).

Polly Bennett | Movement Director

Trained at Royal Central School of Speech. Theatre includes: *The Lehman Trilogy, The Great Wave, My Country; a work in progress, The Deep Blue Sea, Three Days in the Country, Pomona, nut, People, Places and Things* (National Theatre); *As You Like It* (Regents Park); *Travesties* (Menier Chocolate Factory, West End and Broadway); *Salome* (RSC); *Woyzeck* (Old Vic); *The Maids* (Trafalgar Studios); *Yen, Plaques and Tangles, Hang* (Royal Court). TV includes: *The Crown, Killing Eve, Urban Myths.* Film includes: *Bohemian Rhapsody, The Little Stranger, Stan and Ollie.*

Niraj Chag | Composer

Niraj Chag is a London-based composer and artist whose work spans a wide range from albums to film scores, theatre and live events. Credits: *Captive Queen* (Shakespeare's Globe); *Much Ado About Nothing* (RSC); *Rafta Rafta, Dara* (National Theatre). TV includes: BBC1 Oneness ident, Asian Network station sound, *The Secrets of Your Food, Rise of the Continents, Our Girl, Origins of Us, Power of Art, Darwin's Dangerous Idea* (BBC); *Sex and the City* (HBO); *All In Good Time* (Studio Canal).

Helen Atkinson | Sound Designer

Theatre includes: *Grief is a Thing with Feathers* (Complicite); *2nd Violinist, The Last Hotel* (Landmark and Wide Open Opera); *Salomé* (RSC); *Arlington, Ballyturk* (Landmark and Galway International Arts Festival); *The Suicide* (National Theatre); *Much Ado about Nothing* (Queens Theatre, Hornchurch); *You for Me for You* (Royal Court); *The Matchbox* (Galway International Arts Festival); *The Edge, 1001 Nights, As You Like It, Elegy* (Transport); *The Summerbook, 'Twas the Night before Christmas, 1001 nights* (Unicorn Theatre); *NHS@70, Cuckooed and Bravo Figaro* by Mark Thomas (Traverse); *Macbeth* (Cheek by Jowl).

RC-Annie Ltd | Fight Directors

Established in 2005 by Rachel Bown-Williams and Ruth Cooper-Brown, RC-Annie is the UK's leading dramatic violence company. Theatre includes: *Emilia, Othello, The Secret Theatre, Boudica, Lions and Tigers, Much Ado About Nothing, Twelfth Night, The White Devil, Comus, Imogen* (Shakespeare's Globe); *Tartuffe, The Duchess of Malfi, Salomé* (RSC); *A Monster Calls* (Old Vic Productions and Bristol Old Vic); *Common, Ugly Lies the Bone, Peter Pan, The Threepenny Opera, The James Plays* (National Theatre of Scotland and Edinburgh International Festival); *Cleansed* (National Theatre).

Emma Baggott | Assistant Director

Trained at Goldsmiths, University of London, and the Young Vic. Theatre includes, as director: *Normal* (Styx); *The H Word* (Shakespeare in Shoreditch Festival); *Ten Scenes for Women* (Theatre Royal Haymarket); *Scan Artists* (Round House, Brighton Fringe Festival and The Yard). As Associate/Assistant Director: *This House* (UK tour); *McQueen* (Theatre Royal Haymarket); *The Sound of Yellow* (Young Vic); *Tangent* (New Diorama).

Japjit Kaur | Hindi Lyricist and Songs Teacher

Theatre includes: *The Little Match Girl* (Shakespeare's Globe); *Nirbhaya* (international tour); *The Jungle Book* (West Yorkshire Playhouse); *The Empress* (RSC); *Wah! Wah! Girls* (Kneehigh, Sadlers Wells, Stratford East). Film includes: *Amishi*. Vocal MD: *Rafta Rafta*, *Dara*, *England People Very Nice* (National Theatre).

Supporters

We would like to thank the following for their support:

MAJOR DONORS

Scrutton Estates Ltd, The Sahara Care Charitable Trust

VISION COLLECTIVE

Friends Collective: Andrew Grenville, Bakoly Robinson, Hazel Province, Sir Hugh & Lady Duberly, Lady Stratford, Mary Friel, Nick Jakob, Peter & Margaret Hooson, Susan Fletcher, Rt Hon Dame Margaret Hodge MP and all those who wish to remain anonymous

Artists Collective: Barbara Ferris, Caroline Pridgeon, Danielle Whitton, David & Marsha Kendall, Derek Paget, Douglas McArthur, Julian Ashby, Lisa Orban, Pauline Johnson and all those who wish to remain anonymous

Directors Collective: Hedley G. Wright, Rachel Potts for Jon Potts, Hilary & Stuart Williams and all those who wish to remain anonymous

Pioneers: Andrew Cowan, Angela & Stephen Jordan, Elizabeth & Derek Joseph, Nigel Farnall & Angelica Puscasu, Sabine Vinck, Tim Bull & Rosalind Riley and all those who wish to remain anonymous

CORPORATE SUPPORTERS

Devonshires Solicitors, Fresh Wharf Estate, Frogmore, Local Space, Telford Homes Plc.

TRUSTS AND FOUNDATIONS

Allen & Nesta Ferguson Charitable Settlement, The Aziz Foundation   Clifford Chance Foundation Equity Charitable Trust   Esmée Fairbairn Foundation The Foyle Foundation   The Ironmongers Company The Goldsmiths Company   Jack Petchey Foundation Newham Giving Fund   The Rank Foundation Red Hill Charitable Trust   The Rothschild Foundation St James's Place Foundation   Santander Foundation Sir John Cass Foundation   Tesco Bags Of Help Fund The Worshipful Company of Basketmakers

STRATFORD EAST

About Theatre Royal Stratford East

Since 1884, Theatre Royal Stratford East, the historic producing house in the heart of London's East End, has spearheaded diverse work, and championed often marginalised stories on its stage.

From 1953 to 1979 the theatre was the home of Joan Littlewood's legendary Theatre Workshop Company. The Company received international recognition with acclaimed productions such as *Oh, What a Lovely War!* and *A Taste of Honey*.

Many leading actors, writers and directors have been part of the Theatre Royal Stratford East family including Meera Syal, Barbara Windsor, Don Warrington, Sheila Hancock, Indhu Rubasingham, Tanika Gupta, Roy Williams and Cynthia Erivo to name but a few.

Though its innovative Young People's Programme the theatre reaches young people across Newham and beyond, providing access to high quality theatre training, development and artist support.

Artistic Director Nadia Fall delivers a bold programme of reimagined classics, timely revivals and ground-breaking new work that seek to highlight the urgent political issues of our day and reach out to audiences across London.

The Village

April De Angelis's plays include *Wild East* (Royal Court),
A Laughing Matter (Out of Joint/NT/tour),
The Warwickshire Testimony (RSC), *The Positive Hour*
(Out of Joint/Hampstead/Old Vic; Sphinx), *Headstrong*
(NT Shell Connections), *Playhouse Creatures* (Sphinx
Theatre Company), *Hush* (Royal Court), *Soft Vengeance*
(Graeae Theatre Company), *The Life and Times of
Fanny Hill* (adapted from the James Cleland novel),
Ironmistress (ReSisters Theatre Company), *Wuthering
Heights* (adapted from Emily Brontë's novel for
Birmingham Rep), *Jumpy* (Royal Court and Duke of
York's Theatres), *Gastronauts* (Royal Court) and *After
Electra* (Theatre Royal, Plymouth). Her work for BBC
Radio includes *Visitants*, *The Outlander*, which won
the Writers' Guild Award 1992, and *Cash Cows* for the
Woman's Hour serial. For opera: *Flight* with composer
Jonathan Dove (Glyndebourne, 1998), and the libretto
for *Silent Twins* (Almeida, 2007).

Lope de Vega (1562-1635) Spanish playwright and poet,
considered the most influential figure in the Golden Age
of Spanish literature. He sailed with and survived the
ill-fated Armada in 1588, had many passionate love
affairs and two marriages. A prolific dramatist, 470
or so of his plays survive, although he is credited with
as many as 2,000. His *Arte nuevo de hacer comedias*
established the ground rules for the classic Spanish play.

APRIL DE ANGELIS

The Village

after
Fuenteovejuna
by Lope de Vega

FABER & FABER

First published in 2018
by Faber and Faber Limited
74–77 Great Russell Street, London WC1B 3DA

Typeset by Country Setting, Kingsdown, Kent CT14 8ES
Printed in England by CPI Group (UK) Ltd, Croydon CR0 4YY

A CIP record for this book
is available from the British Library

ISBN 978-0-571-35147-3

2 4 6 8 10 9 7 5 3 1

The Village was first performed at the Theatre Royal, Stratford East, on 7 September 2018. The cast, in alphabetical order, was as follows:

Gopi Harki Bhambra
Ishani Sudha Bhuchar
Jyoti Anya Chalotra
Mango Ameet Chana
Ramdev Neil D'Souza
Gina Souad Faress
Panna Rina Fatania
Vihaan Naeem Hayat
Farooq Scott Karim
The Inspector Art Malik
Mekhal / Babu Arian Nik
Jacinta Humera Syed
Ved Ragevan Vasan

Director Nadia Fall
Designer Joanna Scotcher
Lighting Designer Paul Pyant
Movement Director Polly Bennett
Composer Niraj Chag
Sound Designer Helen Atkinson
Fight Directors RC-Annie
Casting Director Amy Ball

Characters

Inspector Gangwar
a corrupt policeman

Ved
a policeman

Gopi
a policeman

Vihaan
a young politician

Jyoti
the Mayor's daughter

Panna
a peasant woman

Farooq
a peasant man

Mango
a peasant man

Ramdev
the Mayor of Sahaspur

Ishani
a progressive Hindu candidate

Mekhal
Ishani's PA

Gina
Co-Mayor of Sahaspur

Jacinta
a peasant woman

Investigator

Townspeople

THE VILLAGE

Act One

SCENE ONE

Airport in Uttar Pradesh.
 Inspector Gangwar and two policemen: Ved and
Gopi.
 They have been waiting.

Gopi
 Where the hell is he? Duty Free?

Ved
 Buying perfume, two bottles; Dolce and Gabbana.
 In Delhi he forgot, but since the death of his pa
 He's not only his girfriend to think of but also his ma.

Gopi
 'It's my prick, sir, it had to take long piss, sir.
 Too much pop on the plane, sir.'

Ved
 Air India has facilities, he should have availed himself!

Gopi
 Better he has a bladder ache than make the Inspector
   wait.
 Student.

Ved
 These small courtesies are the lubrication of business.
 Doesn't he know, sit, you are Gangwar, Inspector of
   Indian Police?
 That should give him some idea of who he is dealing
   with.
 If he knew, he'd be sorry for doing as he wants.

Gopi
 He'd cack his pants.

Vihaan enters.

Vihaan

Inspector Gangwar? The plane took its time to dock.
Apologies. I thought of you waiting, watching the clock.

Gangwar

Do I know you?

Gopi

It's Vihaan, sir. The one we've been waiting for?

Gangwar

Who asked you? Moron.

Vihaan

I should have introduced myself, Vihaan.
I need to grab a coffee, excuse me.

Ved blocks his way.

Ved

Be polite, neh?

Gangwar

Protocol is old fashioned now? I served your father
  twenty years
Perhaps it's self-flattery to expect respect from his son
  for the battles we won?

Vihaan

He relied on your professionalism
His path would have been steeper without your
  wisdom.

Gangwar

Your father was good company.
I was the glove for his fingers or maybe the fingers in
  his glove,
The hidden partner in his political career.
Now sadly a stroke has snatched him from us

And you are here.
Victory seemed certain at the polls but your father's
    passing
Put any celebrations on hold.

Vihaan

It was very sudden.
Though I lit the pyre, saw him consumed by fire
It's impossible to believe he's gone.
The people flocked to his funeral
Crowding the streets, sending heartfelt cries into the
    air,
It seemed the whole of the city was there.

Gangwar

It was well attended, even by his enemies I hear –
Sadly business dictated I could not be spared to
    bestow a final greeting.

Vihaan

You requested a meeting. You need me to sign my
    name, releasing funds for your campaign?
Could you drive me to my hotel?
I'm a little wrung out. I need to get my head down,
    shower.
We could talk mañana?

Gangwar

There's no time for that.

Vihaan

I don't understand.

Gangwar

Your father's plan was that you should enter politics.

Vihaan

Really?

Gangwar

When your studies were done.

Now, a little earlier than he thought, your chance has
   come.
You must be the one to pick up the reins, step into
   the breach.

Vihaan
What, now?

Gangwar
That's why he paid your expensive fees. Not just a
   free ride
But so you could serve your country.

Vihaan
It's just term starts next week.

Gangwar
Forget all that – you're not going back.

Vihaan
Not going?

Gangwar
It seems your stay in UK has left you ignorant of
   what's going on.
There are elections to be won.
Our party, BJP, has sworn to end elite corruption,
Boost national production and our biggest test
Cleansing Hindustan of the Muslim pest.
Perhaps you've been oblivious, buried in your
   university
Leaving us outside to face adversity.

Vihaan
I am completely abreast of contemporary events –
   I'm in the debating society.

Gopi
Good for you. That must get very shouty.

Gangwar
Take his cases.

The policemen go to get his luggage.

Vihaan
I can manage.

Gangwar
We're in a hurry.

Policemen take cases. Vihaan and Gangwar follow.

Vihaan
Where are we going?

Gangwar
Sahaspur.

Vihaan
What's that?

Gangwar
One dusty street and a dog.

Ved
It means courage.

Gopi
That's a joke – It's dead – Nothing goes on in that place –

Ved
But it's strategically placed near the town of Rampur.

Gopi
Win that town, win the state.

Ved
Win that state, win the country.

Both
    India First. Narendra Modi.

Gangwar
    In the quiet little town of Sahaspur, a forgotten
        pocket,
    We will plan our campaign undisturbed.
    The people there are simple, they hold no views
    Leaving us free for what we have to do.
    Welcome to your destiny.

Vihaan
    There's no gain in me raising my voice
    In these matters there's little choice.

    They exit.

SCENE TWO

Sahaspur.
    Jyoti and Panna.

Jyoti
    One wish. The Inspector would leave Sahaspur forever.
    Never come back.

Panna
    Jyoti! Be careful. They say the first sign of falling in
        love is hate.

Jyoti
    Who says that, Panna? What rubbish.

Panna
    It's true. That's what Dimple Kapadia told Rishi
        Kapoor in that old film *Bobby*.

Jyoti
    Never heard of it.

Panna

It's a classic! Blame the brain. Love and hate come
from the same part.
Both make you crazy and both break your heart.

Jyoti

Look at me. I'm about as much in love as that
sheesham tree.

Panna

Oh come on. Everyone likes a man in uniform –
always crisp and neat –
His trousers end at his feet. Who can say 'I'll never
drink from that water'?

Jyoti

I'll never drink from that water. Say I closed my eyes,
swallowed his lies,
Laid back and prayed it was all over. Do you think he
would marry me after?

Panna

No, I don't suppose so.

Jyoti

How many girls are there in Sahaspur that trusted him?
How many have been ruined by him?

Panna

Six.

Jyoti

Taken a walk in the wood and come back all belly
and tears.

Panna

He quite good-looking for an old man of forty. He
has teeth.
There'd be perks – it could be worse.

Jyoti

He's been pestering me for a month. Sending his
goons Ved and Gopi
With pathetic gifts; cashmere shawls and lipsticks.

Panna

Cashmere? No!

Jyoti

Shoes.

Panna

I'd love some shoes.

Jyoti

A new silk kameez.

Panna

New! My grandmother wore these. No one ever sends
me gifts.
Even when I swing my hips like Madhuri Dixit.

Jyoti

Gifts won't change my mind.

Panna

You're so refined!

Jyoti

They went on and on about Gangwar, what a great
man he was.
On and on till I was scared,
But they won't sway me, I'm prepared.

Panna

Where did they say this to you?

Jyoti

Down by the stream where we wash the clothes,
Down by the stream six days ago.

Panna

I wouldn't blame you if you told me you gave in.
They say his house has air-conditioning.

Jyoti

If I want to cool down I'll swim in the stream.
Men are overrated, Panna.
Imagine a lad standing here, and over there
A dish of butter chicken, which would I choose?

Panna

Difficult choice; the dude or the food?

Jyoti

It's no contest.
I'd rather wake at an early hour,
Light the fire, put some naan on it,
Sprinkle sesame on top; devour.
Then at noon I'd rather fry some ghee,
Throw in cumin, gently sauté until its splutters,
Mix in a cup of paneer, spice and powders,
Add the cream add the peas
Eat as I please.
Then at sunset – the best yet: Eggplant Bharta
Roast till its flesh is brown, chop it into bite-size
   chunks
Then fry with ginger, onion and tomato
Season with lemon juice and garam masala.
Doesn't that make your mouth water?

Panna

I'm salivating. My stomach is protesting at being
   kept waiting.
My belly only ever knows half full.

Jyoti

That's why my desire is all for a tasty dish,
Lentil patties with vegetables fried.
I'd go to sleep happy and dry-eyed.

Panna, what I say to you
I'd rather spend my nights with a saag aloo.
Food like this you can trust. It fills your belly,
Leaves you content. It tops lust.
Because once men have had us in the sack
They pass us by and don't look back.

Panna
You're right, Jyoti
When men want you they're like flies.
You can't shake them but when they've had you
Then it's too late – they buzz off after crapping on
    your plate.

Jyoti '
Don't trust any of them.

Panna
That's what I've been telling you all along.
Oh look, here are the boys! Hello!

Enter Farooq and Mango.

Farooq
Mango, honestly, your argument is quite shit.
There's no way I'll go along with it.

Mango
I haven't convinced you then?

Farooq
No, my friend, because your theory is insane,
An undercooked mystery manufactured by your brain.

Mango
Luckily there are some women hanging about who
    can judge for us.

Jyoti
Why should we stick around for a dose of blokes
    explaining?

Panna

Go ahead. I'm up for a bit of entertaining.

Jyoti

Go on then.

Farooq

So, lovely ladies, are you ready?

Jyoti

You're calling us 'ladies', Farooq?

Farooq

Alternative facts. I want to be on trend,
Look at the world; in America –

He flourishes a newspaper.

Trump says the biggest crowds
Cheered him to the White House.
When TV showed it wasn't true
He swore to God he never lied,
Facts just have a different side.
In UK it's 'Austerity's good for the poor,
Cuts in services will give them more.'
Food banks are alternative shopping
Nothing to do with benefits stopping;
In Russia Putin bares his chest
To prove life's better than in the West.
No need to put truth to the test
Ripple those nipples, remove your vest
And how are we here in Hindustan?
In elections we live free from fear
We don't attack minorities here
See that dead man, head beaten in
Alternative facts say he'll live again.
He's alive actually, how does that work?
Alternative facts will drive you beserk.
A Muslim boy fell in love with a Hindu girl,

It was pure love, no question
Troublemakers from the BJP
Swore it was a case of kidnapping
Tore the lovers apart, broke more than their hearts
No matter how hard they tried
To speak their love, everybody said they lied
Because alternative facts weren't on their side.
Ladies, I could go on.

Jyoti

Please don't. I suppose, Farooq, at agricultural college
Your speech would be applauded.
But here in Sahaspur we'll ignore it.
All this stuff you're stressing
Is terminally depressing.

Farooq

Please infect me with your wisdom, Jyoti.

Jyoti

Is a woman supposed to be adoring
When you're being really boring?
Spouting how truth's so diminished
You've turned into a total cynic.
You think we're so gullible and addled
We'll believe any news that's peddled.
So politicians are sparing with the truth,
That doesn't take a genius to compute,
And if those lovers had more than broken hearts
Perhaps they were better off apart.
Your navel-gazing doesn't impress me
Your pompous speechifying won't repress me.
Life goes round as it's always done.
Winter rain, summer sun.
I work in the fields all day
Cutting sugar cane, milking cows, digging with a spade
Then at midday resting up, dozing in the shade.
My back is strong, my legs are steady,

My hands grow the food that will feed my belly.
Why spend your time moaning and whining?
The sun is shining? What a way to experience life!
Your wife, whoever she will be, will sign up to misery.

Mango
She's demolished you. The tongue of a lioness.

Jyoti
Hurry up then. What's your dispute?
We can't stay here all day.

Panna
We can.

Farooq
It's me versus Mango. Basically no contest.

Jyoti
What's Mango been saying now?

Farooq
It's very wrong but he won't admit it.

Mango
Of course not, because I'm right.
Why would I admit I'm wrong when I'm not?

Farooq
He says there's no such thing as love.

Panna
Mango. Love is in every film! Romeo and Juliet –
That's why they killed each other!

Mango
That's not how it happened, Panna.

Jyoti
No love. That's going a bit far, Mango.

Farooq
That's going a bit mad.

Panna

It's probably because he's a bit fat.

Farooq

Love makes the world go round.

Mango

I think you'll find that's angular momentum.

The earth spins because there's nothing to stop it.

Farooq

I'm talking about pyar love like between a girl and boy.

Mango

Yes, okay, there is a kind of natural love that everyone
has.

My hand will protect my face against the slap that
comes its way,

To stop my body getting hurt my feet will put on
a spurt.

When my finger sticks in, my eyelid will close,

As I mis-scratch my nose.

Panna

What's picking your nose got to do with it?

Mango

My point, and I do have one,

Is that no one loves anyone more than they love
themselves.

Panna

Remind me never to fall in love with you, Mango.

I want a passion that's insane.

I want my lover to burn for me like a flame.

Mango

Going out with you would involve some pain.

Panna

You have nothing to worry about, Mango.

I'm after a sexy cane-cutter with a six-pack.

Mango

Isn't that pleasure for the self?

Panna

I hope so.

Mango

See. I hate to crow but I win. There is no love,
Only love of the self. There are no others on the shelf.

Farooq

Jyoti – What do you love?

Jyoti

My freedom, my honour, my papa, my friends, my
    dinner.

Farooq

Nothing else?

Jyoti

No.

Panna

Jyoti would rather eat a biriyani than consider
    matrimony.
For her it's a no-brainer.

Farooq

One day maybe you'll suffer from jealousy, Jyoti.
    I'd like to see that.

Panna

Why's that, Farooq?

Farooq

I have my reasons.

Enter Ved and Gopi, the two policemen.

Ved

Afternoon.

Panna
  Gangwar's men.

Jyoti
  His pimps, you mean.

Farooq
  Ved, still football mad like when you were a kid?

Mango
  And you couldn't afford a ball – just kicked around
    a tin?

Ved
  At training camp we left playground tricks.

Gopi
  We learnt to break bones with sticks.

Jyoti
  What do you want?

Ved
  Is that all the thanks we get, Gopi? After the trouble
    we've taken?

Gopi
  To keep you all secure and safe. Risking our necks.

Farooq
  You've risked your necks for us?

Ved
  Who gave you permission to speak, Farooq?

Gopi
  A son of Mohammad. What are you doing in
    Hindustan?

Farooq
  I live here. This is my home.

Gopi
  I think you'll find that's Pakistan.

Farooq

What's Pakistan got to do with me?

Mango

Anyway it's the same DNA. Church, temple, mosque.
Just houses of God.

Jyoti

Let's go, Farooq.

Ved

This is where the trouble starts with devious Muslims
hiding amongst us.

Farooq

For centuries in broad daylight, living and walking
the streets.

Gopi

How can people live their lives in peace?

Ved

Cows can't live their lives in peace.
Cows are sacred. We Hindus don't eat beef.
Imagine you wake up one day and your cow is gone
But the Muslim beard next door is eating burger with
his son.

Gopi

Something that should not be done.

Ved

An abomination to the Hindu nation.

Gopi

Inspector Gangwar, an honourable man
He heard that things were going down.

Ved

Troublemakers taking over Rampur town.
Fifty miles from here.

So we grabbed our sticks, our guns, the BJP called
  us to arms
To settle the dispute.

Farooq
The BJP betrayed the farmers – won't pay us
For the work we do.
Why would we support you?

Gopi
Mouthy Muslim, aren't you?

Ved
We personally escorted many to hear our candidate
  Vihaan,
He gave a nice preach about foreigners, cows, our
  freedom of speech.
Unfortunately, the Mohammedans kicked off.
We waded in – they had to be stopped.

Gopi
Tell them what happened, Ved?

Ved
By the end a couple of them were – not very well.

Jyoti
Proud of yourselves? Doing Gangwar's dirty work for
  him.

Gopi
Don't bad-mouth the Inspector, he was great.
The night before, he stayed up with us lads till late,
Drank, smoked, cracked a joke,
In the morning, he rolled up his sleeves and entered
  the fray.
Despite his office you couldn't keep him away.

Ved
He looked like a film star – Shashi Kapoor

Not now he's dead but how he looked before.
His uniform ironed to a crisp. Symmetrical the cuffs
    at his wrist.
Bright shining buttons strained over his manly chest.
A roar from his throat primitive and strong.
His stick smashed, splashed droplets of blood
On the white of his collar, his thighs, the streets
As he beat down with love for the people.

Gopi

God willing – come the election, we'll get the results
    we want.
Rampur will be saved.
He's coming now. Receive him with pride.

Ved

Ved and Gopi at his side.

*Gangwar enters with Vihaan and the rest of the
townspeople.*
    They sing to welcome him.

Song.

Gangwar

Residents of Sahaspur,
How much I enjoy returning to this humble place
I bring with me a special guest, Vihaan Mukerjee
The future face of our BJP; Bharatiya Janata; Indian
    People's Party.
We're grateful for the love you've shown us here.

Ramdev

We have only shown a fraction of what we really feel.
Sahaspur and the town council
Who you honour here today
Beg you, a little embarrassed I have to say, to receive
    some modest gifts,
I have commissioned a speech.

Mango
I have it here, Mayor Ramdev. Something I wrote earlier.

Ramdev (*reads*)
'Sahaspur, a hick town, down-at-heel, out of luck
But please do not turn up your nose at our truck
Loaded with sugar cane, rice, pickles, a duck,
With mangoes, lychees and sweets for your larder
A goat, ten chickens, that's just for starters,
Round it all off with a hundred parathas.
It would also mightily please us
If you would accept in tribute some paneer cheeses
Which we offer on bended knees . . . es.
To you and your men, we say, eat, eat, bon appétit.'

Gangwar
You have my gratitude, Mayor Ramdev.

Ramdev
Singers, let's have the song again.

Gangwar
That's not necessary.

Ramdev
No trouble. Please. My daughter will sing,
She has a beautiful voice.
You won't regret the choice.

Jyoti
Baba –

Ramdev
Don't be shy.

Song, which Jyoti sings.

They leave.

Gangwar
You two. Wait.

Jyoti
You mean us, sir?

Gangwar
Who else?

Jyoti
Me and Panna?

Panna
Get lost, Jyoti, not me.

Gangwar
Jyoti, you were insolent to me the other day.

Jyoti
But I've never spoken to you.

Gangwar
You refused the gifts I sent.
Do you make it a habit to offend?

Jyoti
Forgive me, that was not my intent.
It's the way in our village that unmarried girls
Keep to themselves and don't accept gifts from
    strangers.

Gangwar
This is a different case.
I've dedicated my life to keeping you all safe.
Don't I deserve to be shown some respect?

Jyoti
Good day, sir.

Gangwar
Sahaspur wanted to give me more – what do you
    think I should choose?

Jyoti
I'm not sure there's room in the truck for any more, sir.
It's stuffed to the roof as it is.

Gangwar
What if I choose both of you?

Panna
I don't think the mayor meant it like that.

Gangwar
Come inside with me. There we can relax properly.
Get to know each other. Ved?

Ved
Sir.

Gangwar
Encourage the girls to do the right thing and come in.

He exits.

Ved
Don't be stupid girls, get in.
He just wants to tell you tales of Rampur.

Panna
And hear a clang as he locks the door?

Jyoti
Ved, let us pass.

Ved
Cheer up, you've been gifted.
He deserves better than that shit in the truck.

Panna
Gopi. Get out of our way.

Jyoti
Gangwar's had enough meat for today.

Gopi
It's your meat he's interested in.

Jyoti
He'd choke on it. Run, Panna.

They go.

Gopi

Shit. What message do we take to him now?
They both ran off, silly cows. He'll pulverise us.

Ved

It's part of our job as the Inspector's men
To put up with his crap, now and then. Let's go.

SCENE THREE

Ishani, a progressive Hindu candidate standing in the
Rampur election.
Mekhal, her assistant.
They are preparing to go in front of a camera for an
interview.

Mekhal

You're on in five.
Smile, don't be bullied, let them see you're the boss.
Confident you'll win – that's how you'll come across.
One decaf coffee.

He hands it to her.

What colour for your scarf?

Ishani

Does it matter what I wear, Mekhal?
People are surely more interested in what I have to say?

Mekhal

Sometimes I question, Ishani, your sanity.
It's not a question of vanity; Hillary's pant suits,
Angela's blazers, Margaret's handbag, Indira's hair
They're part of the brand, you barely notice they're
    there
But subliminally feel a stab of recognition and so
    sympathise with her position,

A female pays a heavy price if she fails to get her
   outfit right.
Too sexy, too frowsy – if the media start debating
   what she's wearing
It drowns out the message the electorate should be
   hearing.
A woman politician has to sartorially plan.

Ishani

God, it would be easier to be a man.

Mekhal

There's a science to colour – it's a code.
Perhaps we should go for a saffron shade,
Reclaim it from the Hindutva gang?

Ishani

Holy colours worn by self-appointed saints.
You say I must be cool and collected
But I feel the hurt done to innocent people personally.
When my supporters stood up in Rampur
Shouted 'Ishani for farmers' wages and a secular state'
Those fundamentalist nutters couldn't wait to
   bludgeon a few.
Streets ran with blood.
Now fake news, say they were keeping the peace
But the BJP pays for a corrupt police.

Mekhal

Our sources tell us 'Gangwar' in the name they hear.
Ishani, it won't help you to now appear full of
   agitation and fear –

Ishani

It is they that plant fear in people's minds.
Blame me for the riots, point to the bloodshed
And say this unrest awaits our nation
If you vote for Ishani at the polling stations.

The untruth they want to sell to the Hindu majority,
The Congress Party is controlled by a Muslim
    minority.
Our opponents drag us to dark days!
I must speak up!

Mekhal

Stick to the script.
Play your ace – you have blue blood – your father
    a Brahmin
High Caste – that plays well to the Hindu soul –
Keep them on side,
Put the brakes on the populist slide.

Ishani

My country drives me mad – why has everything got
    to be about religion?
Gangwar, where does he reside?

Mekhal

Sahaspur, in the countryside
It's his playground
From there he controls the areas around.

Ishani

The bastard muscle of the BJP!
There's nothing they won't do
To scare off the people of Rampur who would vote
    for me
And so turn it to a victory for Vihaan
Who stands a puppet in his father's place,
A smiling front on the fundamentalist face.

Mekhal

God, one minute to go.
Just remember your three key points.

*Ishani turns on the charm – as if she's looking at
    a camera.*

Ishani
Here are my promises to you:
One – renew economy by building roads for better
    connectivity.
Two – farmers deserve lifesaving subsidy.
Three – ensure religious equality.

Pause.

Four – then we're going to Rampur.

Mekhal
What? On our own – without protection? Even the
    journalists have checked out.

Ishani
I've got to ensure a free and fair election.

Mekhal
It's time. Look straight to camera, don't fidget.
Scarf – go for well-behaved in beige.

Ishani
Mekhal, I've got this down.
Then to Rampur – it will be my town.

They exit.

SCENE FOUR

A wood.
Jyoti and Farooq.

Jyoti
Why have you brought me here, Farooq?
Villagers love to snoop and now you give them
    ammunition
Dragging me to the middle of nowhere.

I left the washing half wrung and came away from the
    river.
You want to 'talk'. Couldn't we have done it without
The boring walk?
You know what the whole village is saying
That you fancy me and I've got the hots for you just
    because
You're not like, really minging. You're okay
But that's mostly because your clothes are marginally
    better
Than the average villager. And that's not hard to
    achieve.
People will be making such a fuss. 'Hindu girl,
    Muslim boy.'
After this there won't be a single person in the village,
    fields or woods
Who won't be whispering that I must be quickly
    married off.
Like that's going to happen!

Farooq

Are you saying you won't marry me?

Jyoti

I'm sixteen. Why would I want to give up my life,
    become a drudge of a wife?

Farooq

Beautiful Jyoti, you're killing me with your words.

Jyoti

It's just how I am.

Farooq

Doesn't it give you a pain to see me practically driven
    insane?
I can't eat, drink, sleep.

Jyoti

See a doctor, Farooq.

Farooq

How can such a hard heart find a place
In such an angelic face?
I just want us to be together, like two doves cooing
and rubbing beaks in harmony.

Jyoti

What's doves got to do with it?

Farooq

Jyoti, you inspire me to poetry.

Jyoti

No thanks. Though I might have a little bit of an
inclination.
Somewhere. If I can remember where I put it.

Farooq

You must have remembered last night. When we
kissed.

Jyoti

That was because of the moon. I wasn't myself.

Farooq

Am I that horrible? Is the thought of us so awful?
Can't you imagine us being together every night?
My definition of total delight.

Jyoti

I can imagine it – that's what I'm worried about.

Farooq

Jyoti.

They hear a noise, look.

The Inspector.

Jyoti

Gangwar, hunting. You hide. It'll be worse if he finds
us together.

Farooq

No. I'm not leaving you alone with that tiger.

Jyoti

I can handle him better alone. Go on. Go.

Farooq hides.

Gangwar

Not bad to be following a timid little buck
And to stumble on such a beautiful doe.

Jyoti

I was having a rest here after washing some clothes
With your permission, Inspector, I'll just go.

Gangwar

Don't refuse my company again.
Can't we be friends?

Jyoti

I've got enough friends, thank you.

Gangwar

I have feelings too, you know.

Jyoti

I can't leave my washing much longer.
It needs to be hung.

Gangwar

Stay a while this won't take long.

Jyoti

Goodbye, sir.

Gangwar

I could name other women in the village who have
Given in to me with very little persuasion.

Jyoti

Maybe they weren't fussy.

ar
ays ready with the sharp tongue.
re's something about you, it's true . . .
I've been chasing you for a month.
Now in this solitary place
You don't have to save face or play hard to get.

Jyoti
Are you going to force me? Have you lost your mind?

Gangwar
Look, I'm putting my gun on the ground.
I'm not going to shoot you, besides there's a practical
reason,
I'm going to need both my hands.

Jyoti
Shiva help me.

Gangwar
Relax or you'll make it worse. It's the right thing.
You'll see.
Then I'll be able to get you out of my head and you'll
be free.

Jyoti
We don't have to do this now – I'll meet you later –
I promise.

Gangwar
No. Let's get this done.

Jyoti
I'll tell everyone.

Gangwar
You're in good hands.

Farooq takes the gun.

Farooq
Inspector Gangwar. Leave Jyoti. Let her go. Jyoti, run.

Jyoti

Farooq!

Gangwar

Bloody dog.

Farooq

Run, Jyoti.

Jyoti

Careful, Farooq.

Farooq

Go.

She goes.

Gangwar

How many men have you killed, cub?

Farooq

I don't want to pull the trigger.

Gangwar

You're going to shoot me? Then do it. I won't turn
    my back.
You'll need to stand up properly – look straight
Down the barrel when you take aim or you'll hit
    a tree.
If you do a bad job I'll be maimed, I'd rather you
    killed me.

Farooq

I'm not going to shoot. I'm quite happy to be alive,
So I'll take the gun and say goodbye.

Gangwar

For this offence and nuisance you will pay.

Farooq exits.

The shame of it. Why didn't I fight him?

He exits.

Act Two

SCENE ONE

Town square.
Ramdev and Gina.

Ramdev

The best way for the town to proceed
Is to take no more rice from our reserves in the store
That is how we manage the need. Other counsellors
    disagree
But having food in stock seems sensible to me.

Gina

Not when people are going hungry!
Gangwar's crew have eaten us out of house and home.
How many times can I serve broth made from a single
    spinach leaf?
We farmers already struggle, the government breaks
    its word
And leaves us drowning in debt – this year is the
    worst yet.
The other counsellors ask us to seek the advice of
    a holy man.

Ramdev

We can't afford a good one – a second-rate fortune
    teller will leave us worse off than before.
They talk the big talk – about fate and stars and
    planetary pulls
How Scorpio is a scorpion and Taurus is a bull
Take our money, treat us like fools;
Tell us where and when to plant our crops,
But they mix it up – the bumpkins! They jeopardise
Our mangoes, sugar cane and pumpkins.

Or they say in a spooky voice 'a cow will die'.
And it does, not here but in Chennai.
I may not be blessed with second sight
But I'll take a punt and say after day comes night.
Will we ever be free of our crippling debts?
They moan and sway and say perhaps you may,
Their gift is prevarication – they're masters of
    equivocation.
About as much use as an earache.

Gina

Okay, well we won't do that then.
The Chaiwallah says Gangwar's men demand a
    private tax
As an insurance against attacks! Extortion!
We've been stripped bare by the Inspector,
He'd take the hair on your arms if you let him
And he's dirty – he pesters the women. Even your Jyoti.
Was there ever anyone so corrupt, so venal?
Me? I'd like to see him hanging from that banyan tree.

Gangwar enters with Ved.

A million thanks to God for you, Inspector.

Gangwar

God keep you, good people.

Gina

Please, sit.

Gangwar

You sit.

Ramdev

No, you sit.

Gangwar

I told you sit. Have you some trouble understanding it?

Gina

Okay, sir.

They sit.

Gangwar
Sahaspur always makes me welcome here.

Ramdev|
We do our best, Inspector. We're humble people.

Gina
We may not be the cleverest or the richest
Or the tallest or the quickest or the finest
Or the sharpest or the bravest or the –

Gangwar
Shut up.

Gina
Yes sir.

Gangwar
The women especially make me welcome here.
There is a one hiding behind her door there
Who gave in to me immediately.

Gina
She was wrong to. May her lettuce droop.

Ramdev
I don't think, sir, you should be talking so liberally.

Gangwar
Liberally? What an eloquent peasant. Ved?

Ved
Inspector?

Gangwar
Let's get down to business.
The Chaiwallah's wife – she's usually up for it.
What did she say?

Ved

That her husband hides her away like rice in a bin
But as soon as she's free you'll be the first one in.

Gangwar

The young widow?

Ved

Definitely, she said – if her husband wasn't so recently
dead.

Gangwar

Panna?

Ved

Getting married – though I can't find anyone who's
claimed her.

Gangwar

She's stalling.
The peasantry is so boring. It's better in the cities.
There men appreciate their wives being visited.
And the women are amenable, don't make such a fuss
They're delighted to be serviced by one of us.

Gina

That can't be true. In cities there must be honour too.

Ramdev

She speaks for me.

Mango enters.

Ved

I like it when women resist.

Gangwar

That's lucky because in your case it must happen a lot.

Mango

Ha ha.

Gangwar

It's true that pleasure in anticipation is ruined if a
woman
Is too forthcoming although it can go too far the
other way.
There is one here who, how can I say, refuses to grant
me a wish.
The offender is your daughter.

Ramdev

My daughter?

Gangwar

Yes.
Rebuke her, Ramdev. She is resisting me.

Ramdev

Inspector, we here in Sahaspur wish to live peacefully
Under your command, sir. You mustn't take away our
honour.

Gangwar

Do you have honour? You let your daughter fraternise
With a Quran–thumper who is ready
To sully our blood with that of his base tribe.

Ved

She's been forced. It's love, jihad.

Ramdev

Not forced.

Gangwar

You say you're concerned to keep your daughter pure.
I found them alone near the river.
A whore is what he'll make of her.

Ramdev

Your words bring dishonour, sir.

Gangwar

Where is Farooq?

Mango

I don't know, sir.

Ved

Skulking somewhere.

Gopi enters.

Gopi

I found your gun, sir. Just left outside your door, sir,
Wrapped up like an old bone, sir.

Gangwar

That peasant takes my gun with impunity?
Was about to kill me. He has the nerve to show his
    face around this place?

Ved

Jyoti is like his bait.
Last night I saw someone who looked like Farooq,
I beat him to a pulp.
But it wasn't him. I made a mistake.

Gangwar

I served this country. I've fought scum.
Now I am threatened by this kid
I don't know what this world's become?
If I wanted to I'd tear this village apart.
(*To Ramdev.*) And you – deliver your daughter to me
    if you know what's good for you.

Vihaan enters.

Gangwar

What is it?

Ve

Vihaan

I've been looking for you.

47

Ishani is heading for Rampur
To hold a rally, playing Mother Teresa,
Telling the people their safety
Will be assured at tomorrow's polls.

Gangwar
Impossible.

Vihaan
She guarantees state police will stand
Armed outside the polling gates
To ensure fair elections.

Ved
Does that mean we are going to lose?

Gangwar
Get this rabble out of the square.

Gina
Dear God, we have to go through this.

Gangwar
Back to your holes like mice.

They leave.

Days of restraint are over. We'll take the risk.
We must ensure those that stand against us
Feel our fist.

They exit.

SCENE TWO

A field in Sahaspur.
Mango, Panna, Jyoti fleeing.

Mango
Ramdev instructed me to take you out of town,
Hide there in the wild till things calm down.

Panna

Mango, this will sound strange:
I'm glad you're with us for a change.

Jyoti

Where's Farooq?

Panna

He risked his life to save Jyoti. It's very romantic.

Mango

A good trick. Only now Farooq is kicking his heels
hiding out here in the fields.

Jyoti

He shouldn't be anywhere near. Why doesn't he
realise he needs to disappear?

Panna

He could apologise maybe? Beg for mercy?

Jyoti

Nothing will change his mind. Gangwar has him
marked.

Jacinta enters.

Jacinta

Please help me.

Mango

It's the untouchable girl.

Panna

She looks petrified. What is she doing outside the
village?

Jyoti

What's your name?

Jacinta

Jacinta.

Jyoti
What's wrong?

Jacinta
They're after me.
The Inspector's men, on their way to Rampur,
Have taken me for their whore. I can't run any further.

Panna
They'll find us too then?

Jacinta
Help me. Hide me.

Jyoti
How can we? Where?
Best we go our separate ways – it's safer.
I need to get to Farooq, persuade him to go.

She exits.

Panna
I'll try that way.

Jacinta
Who will help me?

Panna
Mango will take care of you.

Panna runs off.

Jacinta
Are you armed?

Mango
Two arms.

Jacinta
I wish we had a gun.

Enter Ved and Gopi.

Ved
What are you thinking, running away?

Jacinta
I'm dead.

Mango
Sirs, this poor scrap, a simple Dallit girl – let her go.

Ved
Is this the best you can do, Mango – this shit-shoveller?

Mango
Better a shit-shoveller than an arse-licker.

Gopi
I'll kill him.

Gangwar enters.

Gangwar
What's this?

Gopi
This low-life is protesting, sir.

Gangwar
Really?

Gopi
Shall I stuff his mouth with earth?

Gangwar
No, no, it's worth hearing a citizen's concerns. Go on.

Mango
I have a few suggestions for improvements, sir,
    which I offer up in the spirit of democracy.

Gangwar
And what would those be?

Mango
The constitution of India demands protection of the
    fundamental rights of the people.

Gangwar
Of course.

Mango
In that spirit, sir, punish your men who in your name
Are stealing this woman away from her home.

Gangwar
I've heard what you have to say and I'd rather do it
  my way.
Ved, Gopi, tie his hands.

Gopi
Shall we kill him now?

Gangwar
Don't waste a bullet. Make an example of him.
Take him, tie him to a tree, whip him raw.

Mango
Mercy, sir.

Gangwar
Till he bleeds.

Mango
Sir, have I offended you or had anyone in the town?
  Ved?
My mother had a soft spot for you, remember?

Ved
Shut up, scum. (*To Gopi.*) Shall I whip him while you
  hold him down?

Gopi
Take turns is best. Then when you're tired you can
  take a rest.

They take him away.

Gangwar
You, Dallit girl, why are you running away?
Is a farmer better than a man of my worth?

Jacinta

I didn't want to come – your men dragged me to you.

Gangwar

Dragged you?

Jacinta

I'm a Dallit not fit to clean your shoes, nor drink
    from the same well or cross your shadow's path.
You don't want me – I'll pollute you.

Gangwar

True.

Jacinta

Thank you, sir.

Gangwar

I'll give you to my men. They can use you.

Jacinta

Some pity, sir.

Gangwar

There's no pity in war.

Jacinta

I'll kill myself after.

Gangwar

Whatever. Get moving.

They exit.

SCENE THREE

Gangwar steps in front of Ishani.

Ishani

What are you doing? Get out of my way.

He doesn't.

You're Gangwar.

Gangwar

That's right.

Ishani

Is this police business? It's irregular.

Gangwar

In the flesh you look younger.

Ishani

What do you want?

Gangwar

A personal audience. A one-to-one.
Where are your plans for today?

Ishani

I think you know.

Gangwar

It's polite to ask though.

Ishani

A rally.

Gangwar

Rally. Really. Yes. It's best you don't attend.

Ishani

It seems I have spooked your man, Vihaan,
So he's sent his crooked cop.
Are you frightened I'll come out on top?

Gangwar

We can't guarantee your safety if you attend.

Ishani

A veiled threat. You can't stop me.
Our country is still a democracy. I have a duty to
address the people.

Gangwar

What do you know about the people?

Ishani

I've dedicated to my life to serving them – I'm
  a politician.

Gangwar

My point exactly. A politician. Spawned from the
  Gandhi legacy.
A spoilt rotten dynasty who've never struggled to stay
  alive,
Born suckling a silver spoon. Polished up at the best
  schools.
My father was a landlord of just two rooms.
For what we had we fought.
I took the lessons he taught.
In the dark I woke – hitched to the airport
Brought back the day's papers crumpled, worn
Ironed them, sold them back on the streets
All so the family could eat
And if I was sick, my father would give me a kick
Send me out again
It made me the man I am – did me good.
I never shirk from unpleasant work.

Ishani

Spare me the Bollywood rags to riches.
You and your Modi are still dining out on those sob
  stories?

Gangwar

How is your daughter?

Ishani

My daughter?

Gangwar

Is she enjoying boarding school in Puna? Stay away
  from Rampur
And I'll make sure nobody touches her.

Ishani

I'll call the law on you.

Gangwar

I am the law.

Now kiss me on the forehead like my father used to
when I was a good boy.

He exits.
Mekhal enters.

Ishani

Where the hell were you, you bastard?

He leaves.

SCENE FOUR

Town square.
Jyoti and Farooq.

Jyoti

Why have I let you take me home, Farooq?

Farooq

The safest place is here. Gangwar is in Rampu,r
Maybe someone will do us a favour, finish him off
there.

Jyoti

Hold off the curses, people tend to live longer
When you wish death on them.

Farooq

In that case may he live forever.
This buys us some time, Jyoti – be mine.

Jyoti

Farooq – you should have left by now.

Farooq

I want to be where you are.

Nothing else makes sense to me.
You draw me – like the moon draws the sea.

Jyoti

Have you gone completely crazy? You held a gun up
to the Inspector's chest – he won't let that rest.
I don't know how to get that into your head.

Farooq

You love me though, don't you?

Jyoti

Go, why don't you?

Farooq

I gave him back his gun.
Perhaps now Gangwar will leave us alone.
An old married couple.
Don't keep me waiting.

Jyoti

There was supposed to be time – to be young –
have some fun.

Farooq

Marry me, Jyoti, and I'll promise I'll go – I'll run.
Is it because you don't love me?

Jyoti

That's not it at all.

Farooq

So will you?

Jyoti

Yes, if it means you'll go.

Farooq

Let me kiss you for this vow.

Jyoti

Here's my father now – ask him – before I change
my mind.

Enter Ramdev and Gina.

Ramdev
Gangwar has overstepped the bounds.
He has always been corrupt, a tyrant,
But never before has he sunk this far down.

Gina
For a while we can breathe – he's out of town.
He takes girls from the streets.
I'm barely safe in my widow's weeds.

Ramdev
He whipped Mango too.

Gina
No black cloth or ink is as dark as his flesh now.

Ramdev
Don't say any more.
What is the point of our office
If we are so powerless?

Gina
We must go to the temple – pray for better times.
Prayer is the only weapon we have in our hands.

Enter Farooq.

Farooq
It's Farooq, sir.

Ramdev
Has that madman Gangwar done you wrong?

Farooq
That's not why I've come. I hope you'll be happy.
I've come to ask to join your family.

Ramdev
To join?

Farooq

I'm making so bold as to ask to become Jyoti's husband.

Gina

Muslim boy. Who will marry them, Pundit or Imam?

Farooq

I'd walk round your temple fire
If it would join us forever.

Ramdev

Your father was a good man.
Your grandfather's built the village well.

Gina

The women brought the stones
The men dug down
Until they hit the water that runs beneath our town.

Ramdev

To join? Hindu and Muslim.
Everyone will want their say, this is a problem
    that won't ever go away.

Farooq

I know.

Ramdev

As to my Jyoti, I admit wanted a son.

Gina

But unluckily it was a girl that came.

Ramdev

From the first minute I saw her
She had my heart, my daughter.

Gina

He gave out sweets, ludoos and burfi,
And we all said, what's up with him,
He's smiling and it's not a son
Perhaps it's the pain has made him deranged.

Ramdev

But they were wrong
And when her mother was gone
She was the one who looked after me, the light of
    my eyes.
I am happy to accept any son who protected her
As you have done. But the decision is Jyoti's.

Gina

It's a girl's duty if her father accepts the suitor.
Woman must obey man.
My husband's dead, God rest him.

Ramdev (*he calls her*)

Daughter.
She has a sharp tongue, she'll lay down the law.

Farooq

I'm a modern man – I expect my wife to answer back.

Gina

Now you say that.

Ramdev

If she agrees, we can talk dowry.

Farooq

You don't need to.

Gina

Has no one told you before
It doesn't help a couple to be poor?

Ramdev

Jyoti my love, come over here.
It's been a heavy day but now
Farooq has asked me – tell me if you think this is
    right –
That he be given to your good friend Panna
For his bride.

Jyoti
Panna?

Ramdev
You think she's too good for him?

Pause.

Exactly, that's why I thought he'd be better off
marrying you. The one with the big feet.

Jyoti
You're still making bad jokes at your age?

Ramdev
Do you love him?
You want me to say yes.

Jyoti
Say it for me, Father.

Ramdev
Farooq – you're in luck – Jyoti will have you. And
about the dowry.

Farooq
You're offending my honour.

Jyoti
No, he's not, Farooq. We're taking it.

Gina
Don't say I didn't warn you.

Ramdev
Son,
She'll start as she means to go on.

Ramdev and Gina exit.

Jyoti
What's up now, Farooq? You're not crying?

oy.

I reel so good, Jyoti, when I look at you
Seeing you look at me the same way too.

They exit.

SCENE FIVE

A sleazy bar near Rampur.

Vihaan
She's won. Disaster.
I thoughr you said you warned her off?
Instead she was inspired.
She spoke with redoubled eloquence.
She shamed us. Blamed us for the riots.

Gopi
It's a tragedy.

Ved
Our support really flagged
Even the garlands sagged.

Vihaan
People, she said. I'm scared but I'm here.
Her supporters flocked to sign, those illiterates pressed
their inked thumbs
Beside her name.
The ragbag of independents joined forces and taking
her side
Drowned us in an electoral landslide.

Gangwar
I might as well go.

Vihaan
What? There's no new plan?

Ved

We're going to leave, Vihaan?

Vihaan

You dragged me to this place
Paraded my father's legacy, made me see
My duty.
You persuaded me to make this journey
Only to abandon me?
Now when the fire begins to burn in my belly
Calling me to liberate my country?
Now he tells me!

Gangwar

Vihaan, lick your wounds, look to the next day.
I'll go home, unfinished business awaits me there.
You're young, the lesson is hard won,
The game of politics is a devious dance
You bear the knocks, await the budding chance.
We lost the battle not the war.
Now I've skulls to crack in Sahaspur.

SCENE SIX

The wedding.

Song.

Panna

What a gorgeous song.

Mango

They didn't spend that long writing it though, did they?
Repetitive, I'd say.

Panna

Have you got a romantic bone in your body, Mango?

Mango

I'm 60 per cent chapatti – and I'm happy with that.

Farooq

Go on then, Mango – show them what you're made
of – you sing.

Mango

I'm not in the mood for singing – I've had my buttocks
  whipped
So soundly it's taken the spring from my step.
Also they also stuffed an enema up my arse.

Panna

Oh God, less is more, Mango.

Mango

That's what I said as I shat myself.

Farooq

That's how they get their laughs?

Mango

I laughed till I cried, till I was empty inside.

Panna

Oh well, look on it as a spiritual cleansing.

Mango

Can't see it catching on.

Farooq

You complain about the song, Mango – but are you
  all talk?
Could you do any better>

Mango

I pray to Bagwan the happy couple
Manage to avoid the usual trouble
At first everything is perfect, rosy
Then one day she thinks, oh lordy
How many times has he told that story?

She wishes they could afford a new mat
He thinks oh why has the sex has gone flat
Last year he swore to mend the chair
She sat on it – her arse went into the air
She fed his dinner to the dog
He sits outside on his favourite log
That pleases them both I'm afraid to report
Cos the person that most annoys them now
Is the one with whom they took their vow
Hopefully this won't happen to you
Because you're my friends
But don't count on it.

Farooq
Pure poetry.

Panna
Your poem is like a doughnut.

Mango
How do you figure that out?

Panna
Or like a jalebi.
You took some dough, threw it in the burning oil
Some bits came out too crispy, some bent
Some burned, a waste of the time you spent.
That's the same way you composed your verse
The pan is the paper, dough the words,
Your hope is the music, like syrup will cover over
The stupid shapes you laid out on the plates
But the only one to eat them will be you.
Because it's only for a tone-deaf person they'll do.

Farooq
Bravo.

Panna
No problem.

Mango

A bit of a poet yourself, Panna, on the sly.

Panna

I try.

Song.

Enter the Inspector with the policemen.

Ramdev

You've come in uniform. Why have you come, sir?
Would you like to sit, sir?

Farooq

I'm dead.

Jyoti

Run, Farooq. Run away.

Gangwar

There's the criminal that stole my gun, threatened me
    with it.
Take him.

Ved

Give yourself up.

Farooq

So you can beat me?

Gangwar

I'm not the sort of man to beat people for no reason,
I represent the law, else these men with me
Would, by now, have smashed you up against a wall.
I've come to take you to prison.

Panna

Sir, he's getting married.

Gangwar

So what he's getting married? What's that to me?

Gina

If he offended you, sir, forgive him
Prove a generous man.

Gangwar

He's a terrorist. Ved, Gopi – take him.

Jyoti

No!

Ramdev

It's not surprising that a young lover will try to protect
The woman he's in love with –
You were trying to have your way with his wife
And so he risked his life for her. Spare him, sir.

Gangwar

You're a fool, Mayor.
She wasn't his wife then. You're quick to give your
consent to it.
But are you sure she wasn't forced?
This Muslim scum surely used ill methods
Stealing our Hindu women is a way of humiliating us.

Ramdev

No, you're wrong.
I know my daughter, nothing could persuade her
Except love.
As to our community – we have always lived together
in peace,
Hindu, Muslim, Christian, Sikh –

Gangwar

Islam is a foreign religion. Barbarians brought it here –
It's not even Indian.
Take away his staff of office. He's unfit.
This place needs to be purified of multicultural shit.

Ramdev

Take it, please.

Gangwar

Bring the prisoner.

Jyoti

Leave him alone. What is he guilty of? Protecting
my honour?

Gangwar

Not even wearing a clean kurta to his own wedding.
You're too good for him, Jyoti.
Think of the mongrel children he would father.

Jyoti

I'm marrying him –
And I'll love him and have him night after night for
the rest of my life.

She kisses Farooq.
Gangwar pulls her off Farooq.

Gangwar

Take him away.

Jyoti

You're obsessed. Farooq!

Farooq

Jyoti.

They take Farooq away.

Jyoti

Here I am dressed as a bride with no husband by
my side.
Perhaps you think I should marry you?
Except that you disgust me.

Gangwar

Slut.

He puts his hand forcibly down Jyoti's top. It rips.
Ramdev averts his gaze. Jyoti gives a cry.

Jyoti
Father! Baba! Don't let them take me. Baba!

They take her.

Gangwar (*to Ramdev*)
Perhaps you'd like to watch?

Gangwar, Gopi, Jyoti exit.

Ramdev
Where is justice?

Gina
The wedding's turned to mourning.

Panna
What can we do?

Mango
Say nothing – they have guns and my welts still feel
the whips.
Let that seal our lips.

We hear a last scream from Jyoti.

They exit.

Act Three

SCENE ONE

Jyoti enters. She is unrecognisable.
  She rings the bell. Slowly the villagers emerge.

Panna
  Jyoti? Is that you?

  The village gathers.

Gina
  Better she had died than come back alive
  To face the shame.
  The sin will stick to her, make her hide her face
  Impossible to live with that disgrace.
  Don't touch her. Bad luck can spread by touch it is
      said.
  It's a bad omen for the village.
  Better off if in the extremity of her grief
  She had killed herself.

Panna
  It's like a ghost of Jyoti has come back.

Ramdev
  Is that my Jyoti?

Gina
  That was her lovely wedding dress that we sewed.
  Torn now.

Panna
  How can we help her?

Gina
  We'd all like to – but if someone does
  We may yet feel the Inspector's wrath.

Ramdev

Oh help me. It is my daughter.

Jyoti

Don't call me that.
You let Gangwar's thugs take me
And you stood, soft-limbed, like children
Shuffling, staring, I'll never wipe from my mind
The expressions you were wearing – stunned-eyed
And weak. The men of Sahaspur, what a pitiful bunch
Of cowards you are – as I was marched away
In their vicious grip to be raped and raped.
Doesn't my hair tell its own story?
Or my bloody clothes, my wedding dress of rags
Or my beaten face which was used as a
Space to smash their fists
While they drove into me with their sex
Till my mouth was dry of any cry
Because who would hear it?
Are you my father?
I was your daughter, not yet Farooq's wife
You had the responsibility to protect my life.
Don't you writhe inside to see my pain?
Sahaspur – means courage – never has a town been
So misnamed. It should burn with shame.
Stones, sheep, mice, worms
Yes, that's what you're like – worms –
Blind and buried in the earth, too scared of the bird's
  sharp beak to take a peek,
Too timid to raise a shriek
Tigers would pursue anyone who harmed their young
Rip them apart with teeth and tongue
Instead you let us women, helpless, be taken, fucked,
  shouldered like sheaves,
While you stood hanging by like rotten leaves.
Tomorrow, Gangwar plans to hang Farooq
No trial, no verdict

Maybe one day his body will be found
Maybe it will never be found.
Gangwar then will turn his vengeance on these half-men
Pick them off one by one. That will do us a favour,
    women –
Because when we are purged of them
We can be Kalis, warrior women – who drink our
    enemies' blood
We have no need for these eunuchs
Better we are alone – a new race to take their place.

Ramdev

Daughter, don't speak like this
My grey hair is bathed in tears.
Jyoti means light.
And now they've snuffed it out.

Jyoti

Don't be deceived, none of you are safe
I may not be the first
But I will not be the last,
This pitiless man
Has an insatiable appetite
To inflict a terrible price on every life.
Nothing is sacred, he'll keep going till
There's nothing left to take
Till we are reduced to slaves.
You have a choice – to resist,
And face this calamity together
Or to submit. Don't make that error.
Let us fight!
What are we waiting for? Pick up your weapons
The stones from the streets.
The tools from our kitchens, our farms
Shall be our arms.

Ramdev

We men will go – march on the gaol.

Mango

Demand they set Farooq free.

Jyoti addresses the women.

Jyoti

Women, why are you sitting?
Knitting, kneading, suckling
While between my legs a fire burns and in my brain
    the thought is churning
What can remove this pain, my honour's stain?
Can't you see how they are all going to finish
    Gangwar?
All the men.
When it's us women who've been the most wronged?

Gina

What can we do?

Jyoti

We have hands, we can pick up stones
To sate the vengeance nestling in our bones.
Jacinta, you're my sister in violation
We can all be a troop of women.

Jacinta

I'm with you, Jyoti.

Panna

Me too.

Gina

And me.
I'll turn my widow's weeds into a banner
And march with you.

Jyoti

We are all in this together.

Ramdev

Let's speak in one voice

This way of life has to end.
Death to the tyrant.

All

Death to the tyrant.

They go.

Farooq sits with his hands tied.
  Gopi, Ved, Gangwar. Gangwar is drinking.

Gopi

There's a lot of bloody noise out there.

Ved looks out of a window.

Ved

There's a protest, sir.

Gopi

The whole village is here.

Ved

It's what they call a popular uprising.

Gopi

They appear quite angry.

Loud smash.

Ved

They're trying to smash through the door.

Gopi

Is that serious, sir?

More noise.

Farooq

I could talk to them.

74

Gopi

Piss off.

More noise, shouting.

Ved

Sounds like they want you, sir – but not in a good way.

Farooq

Ved, lad, It's me they want. You could let me go.
I could talk them down.

Ved

That's a good plan, sir, they appear to mean war,
They've definitely smashed though the outer door.
Farooq. Mate. You have a chance now to live.
Very straightforward. Show your face, tell them to go home.
Then you can expect some leniency to be shown.

Gopi

Is that a good idea? He could fuck off.

Ved

Got a better one, shit for brains?
Remember it'll work out badly for you if you try anything.

He lets him go.

They'll turn back when he talks to them. They're weak.

Gopi

But what if they don't?
They feel power for once and it goes to their heads?

Ved

I know these people – I'm from here –
They're not the fighting type, no fear.

*They sit and listen to shouts, noise of smashing.
Outside, the women gather.*

Jyoti

Women – we have to go in.

Gopi

Bloody noisy out there. That bloody Muslim bastard
is doing a shit job.

We should have hung him when we got the chance.

Ved

Sounds like they've broken through the door. What
do we do?

Gangwar

We fight. We're men. Not like those creatures we're
pitted against.

Dogs, pigs, Dallits all in tow. Let's gp.

Noise from inside.

*At that moment Gopi runs out. Followed by Farooq
and Mango.*

SCENE THREE

Office in Rampur.
Ishani and Mekhal.

Mekhal

They went too far. The villagers took the law into
their own hands.

Gangwar is dead.

Ishani

I would have liked a front seat. Is that something
I shouldn't have said?

The women led the assault apparently

Tearing at his flesh with their bare hands, like modern
day Bacchante –

Mekhal

>Gripped by a primitive rage – closer to the surface
>in the lower classes –
>These witches ripped him to shreds with harsh cries,
>screams and cheers.
>His largest remaining organs were, they say, his ears.

Ishani

>They were angry obviously. Allegedly he was a rapist –
>We all he knew he was a creep.

Mekhal

>I think you have to be careful that no one outside
>of these four walls
>Considers you anything less than totally appalled.

Ishani

>He was my enemy and although I can pretend to grieve
>I feel relieved. They've done me a favour.

Mekhal

>One slip by you over this whole debacle
>And I won't need to consult my oracle. You'll be
>political toast.
>You must say at the first opportunity he was a great
>man.

Ishani

>That would make me a hypocrite?
>Still, I must play the politician and say I'm very sorry.

Mekhal

>What's more, you must demand the state brings the
>perpetrators to light,
>If not, it gives ammunition to the BJP who will spin
>this as
>This as a Hindu–Muslim war and you on the side of
>the terrorists.

The ripples from this heinous act have caused the
  country to react.
It could be the kindling that sets us alight. Riots and
  unrest
May rock India, bring her to the brink of civil war.
It's happened before. In Gujurat – where
  violence
Was stirred by Modi's lies and thousands died on
  either side.

Ishani

It won't come to that.
Sahaspur is a sleepy little town – a pimple on a pimple.
Relax, Mekhal, news is an invesigator has been
  dispatched
Hopefully that will be the end of that.

SCENE FOUR

The village.
  The morning after the night before.
  Jyoti wears Gangwar's jacket smeared with blood.

Panna

Mercy, he cried, and then we stamped on his insides.

Laughter.

Now his blood has dried on our clothes
But the smiles are still on our faces.
I kept one of his ears.
Here.
You're quiet, Jyoti. Want to hold it?

Jyoti

No.

Panna

What's wrong with you?

Ramdev
Daughter, is there something on your mind?

Jyoti
Sahaspur – listen to me.
The law will come to investigate soon.

Panna
Why don't they just leave us alone?

Jyoti
Because we killed –

Farooq
A beast.

Mango
In uniform.

Jacinta
Three, actually.

Jyoti
One of them Gangwar.

Gina
I was only guarding the door.

Panna
And I'm a Kareena Kapoor.

Ramdev
Jyoti is right. We must come to our senses, face facts.

Farooq
What can we do?

Jyoti
They'll call us a mob.

Panna
I'm not a mob.

Jacinta
    Me neither.

Mango
    As if?

Jyoti
    Say we got drunk on the drug of disorder,
    Put us in gaol – throw away the key.

Gina
    Foreboding is growing in me.
    People like us never get away with anything.
    You have to be powerful to commit a crime and
        walk free.
    And that's not a poor widow like me.

Panna
    Will there be rats in prison?

Gina
    Giant ones with sharp teeth.
    When you sleep – they eat your feet.

Mango
    A city gaol. Misery. I like to sleep under the stars.
    Now I'll wake to prison bars.

Panna
    What did we do it for?
    We'll be worse off than before.

Jyoti
    They'll want to know who struck the first blow –

Gina
    Threw the first stone –

Jacinta
    Pushed in the first blade –

Panna

What a crazy way we behaved.

Jyoti

I don't want to be separated from you, Farooq.

Farooq

Jyoti, we'll do whatever you think.

Jyoti

If we stick together
When they ask us 'What was it for,
Who did the killing?'
Our answer shall be
Sahaspur.
They can't arrest a whole village
Let's make a pact – we'll all be in it
We'll all say Sahaspur did it.
Are we agreed?

All

Yes. We agree.
We'll do it.
It's the only way.

Jyoti

People of Sahaspur. Are we agreed?

All

Yes, yes.

Ramdev

I'll be the investigator, we can practise what we'll do.
Mango, we'll start with you?

Panna

They're bound to grab you first, Mango, because
there's more of you.

Mango

Okay, I'm ready. Bring it on.

Ramdev

Mango.

Mango

That's me, right.

Panna

Yes go on. And say it nice and loud like you're in the movies.

Just imagine I'm Katrina Kaif and you're Akshay Kumar.

Mango

There's a limit to my imagination, Panna, and you pushed it too far.

Panna

I hope they pull your balls off.

Ramdev

Who killed Gangwar?

Mango

Sahaspur.

Ramdev

Break his fingers.

Panna

They wouldn't do that?

Mango

Do what you like, I won't confess.

Ramdev

So again – who killed him?

Mango

Sahaspur did.

Farooq grabs Mango from behind.

Farooq

Who was it?
This isn't a game.

Mango shrieks.

Mango

It wasn't me – I mean it was me plus everyone here.
Sahaspur.

Gina

They're here. They've come.

SCENE FIVE

The Investigator, his men and Vihaan.

Vihaan

This was a political assassination. The perpetrators
    must be found.
Root them out.
Don't let the guilty go to ground.

Investigator

They'll confess. A crime like this won't go undetected.

Vihaan

A town of savages –

Investigator

We will handle it – the law is clear. We'll find
    the culprits.
We won't tolerate evasions. If we have to
We'll employ extra-judicial persuasions.

Vihaan

Do what you have to do.

Vihaan watches as the Villagers are brought on.
    The Villagers await their turn in the queue for
interrogation.

*Each person for interrogation is taken behind the
Villagers – they are not allowed to look round but are
forced to hear the interrogation knowing that their
turn is next.*

Jyoti
Farooq –

Farooq
Jyoti –

Jyoti
I'm scared too you know.

Farooq
Take care, Jyoti – that's all I care about.

Panna
How can she do that? We're all in for it.

Mango
I thought the rehearsal was bad.
You'll be okay, Panna –

Panna
Shut up, Mango.

Ramdev is taken.

Jyoti
My father's first.

Farooq
Jyoti. Be strong.

Gina
Are they going to torture an old man?

Investigator
Tell us the truth
Who killed Gangwar?

Ramdev
Sahaspur.

Investigator

What? I know where we are. I was asking who did it?

Strikes him.

Ramdev

Sahaspur.

Farooq Your father is strong.

Investigator

I know you know who did it. Tell me?
Not saying, old man?

Ramdev cries out as he is hit.

Investigator

Who killed him?

Ramdev

Sahaspur.

Investigator

Enough. He's lost his mind. Now that woman.

Panna

Oh God, it's my turn.

Jyoti

Sister – be strong.

Mango

Be brave. What am I saying? I won't be able to stand
it myself.

Investigator

Do not doubt that I will get the truth out.

Jyoti

He's enjoying this.

Investigator

Who killed the Inspector?

Panna
Why are you asking me, sir?

She cries out.

Sahaspur.

Investigator
Is this some kind of joke?

Jyoti
Panna isn't talking, Farooq.

Investigator
Come on – just tell us who killed the Inspector,
Then you can go home and cook your dinner.

Panna
I told you before, Sahaspur.

Investigator
Give her some more pain.

Jyoti
You won't break Panna.

Panna screams.

Investigator
Who was it?

Panna
Sahaspur.

Investigator
Get that one.

Mango
Shit.

Farooq
Mango will confess.

Mango cries.

Investigator
Put your back into it.

Mango cries.

Tell me – who killed Inspector Gangwar?

Mango
I'll tell you –

Jyoti
No, Mango –

Investigator
Squeeze it out of him.

Mango
Stop, I'll tell you.

Investigator
Who?

Mango
Sahaspur, sir.

Investigator
Get rid of him.

Jacinta
They've taken little Ramu – snatched him from his
    mother's arms.

Jyoti
He's just a child.

Investigator
Now tell me – you know – and it will go badly for
    you if you don't tell the truth
Who killed Inspector Gangwar?

The child screams.

Investigator
Are you going to let me hurt a child? Speak up for
him, one of you. Are you human?

All
Sahaspur Sahaspur Sahaspur.

Vihaan looks like he is about to be sick. Exits.

Investigator
These shits have weak stomachs.
Let's call it quits. We tried, there was much at stake
But Sahaspur won't break.

*Disgusted with the whole process, the Investigator
exits.*

SCENE SIX

Ishani, Mekhal, Vihaan.

Mekhal
Vihaan's here. I told you this day would come.

Vihaan enters.

Ishani
Vihaan. To what do we owe the privilege?

Vihaan
Ishani.

Mekhal
Can I get you some tea?

Vihaan
No thanks. This thing in Sahaspur –

Ishani
Condolences. I won't lie,
Say Gangwar and I saw eye to eye – but one

Has to respect one's opponents – though I'm not sure
What he thought of me.

Vihaan

He didn't say.

Ishani

Maybe it was the best way. He was a great man.
Nonetheless – the women of India have been protesting
  in support of Sahaspur.
They feel his death was justified.
Yes, it's been an outpouring of suppressed rage –
  hashtag MeToo.

Vihaan

That's half the story – the rest is a policeman died
  on duty.
There's outrage on the streets that more than meets
  the women's cries.
I never wanted to stand. It was always my father's
  plan – not mine.

Mekhal

You lost the election, you're a free man.

Vihaan

But then Gangwar's death set me right.
My father's man torn apart and what's his crime?

Ishani

Multiple rapes, I think.

Vihaan

He was never convicted in a court of law.
This is bigger than I had thought before.
A historic moment for our country and my father's
  party.
You may have won here, but you don't have the
  country.
Now I feel it is my destiny to fight on.

Ishani

He's drunk the Kool-Aid.

Vihaan

Will you bring the perpetrators to justice?

Ishani

The village is sticking together – they won't point the
finger at a single ringleader.

Vihaan

Punish the whole village if you must
Or face the consequences in the courts.
The headline: 'Hindu man torn apart by a Muslim
crowd'.
I'll fight you all the way on this. My father's man.
A good man.

Ishani

They have his ears apparently. Although I also heard
That was a euphemism for his cock
Which the women bit off.

Mekhal

Ishani –

Vihaan

This is a mockery. You haven't heard the end of this.

He exits.

Mekhal

Really, was that politic?

Ishani

They killed a rapist.

Mekhal

An *alleged* rapist.
As the minister of Rampur in a story this big
You could either advise that the court pardons them –
Or rather condemns the villagers to death –

If you're seen to be merciful
It gives your enemies the leverage to say
You wanted Gangwar done away.
Be warned if the BJP brings you to court
Accuses you of complicity – their pockets are deep.
And if you're found guilty of terrorist support – you'll
    lose your seat
Face irreversible political defeat. He's right.
There must be a reckoning in Sahaspur.

Ishani

Well, that's where I'll go

Mekhal

What? Why?

Ishani

I have to look them in the eye.

SCENE SEVEN

Sahaspur.
   They gather round Mango.

Panna

Mango. Why don't you sit down?

Mango

I'd rather stand due to circumstances beyond my
    control.

Panna

Mango. You were brave.

Mango

And so were you.

Panna

It's almost like we were in a film. The friends of the
    main characters.

Overlooked, but way more fun, and we get together
   in the end.

Mango
   I'd like to see that film.

Ramdev
   What shall we say to Ishani?

Gina
   We should feed her.
   I've made a nice chicken biryani.

Mango
   I'll say I'm Mango – how do you do - I'm a poet too.
   I've written one in your honour.

Panna
   Don't read it – you'll send her to sleep
   And at the worst – prejudice our case with your verse.
   Just get on with it, my love.

Mango
   All right, petal. I'll say
   That I tried to defend this young woman, Jacinta,
   From his people – who wanted to force her – then kill
      her
   Then two men set upon my
   Buttocks with such savagery – one each – that I
      practically had to have surgery.
   I have spent on this prodigious attack money that I'll
      never get back
   For ointment fortified with sulphide.

Panna
   Which I've been applying to his backside.

Mango
   I'll say this much. Panna has a special touch.

Ramdev

We'll ask for clemency – and hope that she will see
    mitigation in this case.
Here she comes.

Enter Ishani and Mekhal.

Ishani

So this is Sahaspur
Are these the aggressors? They don't look like
    murderers.
You can see my predicament –
Although I can believe these stories of corrupt police
I can't recommend your release from these charges.
There is no proof of what you assert – it's hearsay,
A man is dead and someone must pay.

Jyoti

What do you advise people like us to do?
We are the forgotten, the faceless,
No one was sent here to help us,
So we suffered that brute and one day we stood up
Like people not beasts and said no.
We women avenged ourselves.
We want to know – Do you stand with us?

Ishani

Vigilante justice is not something I can trust.
It's never a legitimate way to proceed.
A politician can't be seen to concede.
Gangwar was never charged in a court of law,
And so he was innocent.

Jyoti

He was guilty.

Mekhal

Not technically.

Ishani

You can't ask that I endorse brute force – for in future
times
What would protect us from being a victim of its
crimes?

Jyoti

But when the law is corrupt, then what?
When justice is impossible because savage force rules
Isn't it our duty to oppose, not stay tyranny's fools?
To fight for our lives, and the rule of law too?
How can you say that's the wrong thing to do?
How can right prevail if people do not take risks
To ensure it exists? Are we supposed to submit to evil?
Obeying the law of a lawless devil?
We villagers said if no one will fight for us
Then we will fight for ourselves – our dignity
Own the right to live decently.
Isn't that what you want for your daughter?
Aren't we your daughters too?

Ishani

That's true –
Mekhal. Where there's no one culprit I can't advise a
sentence.
That's the law.
The whole town can't be arrested – it's ridiculous that
that's suggested.
No matter how awful the crime – this time it must be
pardoned.
These people of Sahaspur will continue their lives
as before.
And I hope the country sees my point of view.
What's the point of power unless sometimes you do
The right thing.

The Villagers begin to sing in celebration.

Mekhal – have I blown it?

94

Mekhal
What can you do now but own it?

Song.

Farooq
So – who really did kill him?

Jyoti
Sahaspur.

Farooq
The truth now.

Jyoti
You're scaring me now. Sahaspur.

Farooq
And me – what did you kill me with?

Jyoti
With loving you too much.